THE DEATHLESS
PARAGON

THE DEATHLESS
PARAGON

JOSE GARAY RELATIVO

Copyright © 2019 by Jose Garay Relativo.

ISBN:	Hardcover	978-1-7960-0844-9
	Softcover	978-1-7960-0843-2
	eBook	978-1-7960-0842-5

All rights reserved. No part of this book may be reproduced or transmitted in any form or by any means, electronic or mechanical, including photocopying, recording, or by any information storage and retrieval system, without permission in writing from the copyright owner.

Any people depicted in stock imagery provided by Getty Images are models, and such images are being used for illustrative purposes only. Certain stock imagery © Getty Images.

Print information available on the last page.

Rev. date: 11/20/2019

To order additional copies of this book, contact:
Xlibris
1-800-455-039
www.Xlibris.com.au
Orders@Xlibris.com.au
804427

CONTENTS

The Last War On Earth 1
The Man Who Set The World On Fire 2
The Supreme Manifesto 3
The Veredical Marque 4
Bring On The Truth Instead 5
The Pain Of God 6
Heroine 7
The Spiteful World 8
Truth In The Song 9
The Birth Of Wisdom 10
Heaven Hails Reason 11
Ode To Beauty 12
The End Times 13
Sapienta 14
The Lionhearted Principle 15
Emptiness Through The Door 16
The Drizzle Over The Rain 17
The Great Tribulation 18
Drunk On Your Tears 19
The Castle Of Your Heart 20
The Liquor Of The Mind 21
Under Starlit Heavens 22
God Cometh 23
The Deified Ancestry 24
Into My Arms 25
Godforsaken 26
The Apocalyptic Union 27
Certain Of His Lent 28
Your Face In A Song 29
The Resignation Of Love 30
The Immaculate 31
The Bloodiest Eclipse 32

Title	Page
Beauty Like Death	33
Ace Of Pain	34
The Thief In The Night	35
The Most Beautiful Song	36
Trampling On Fate	37
Bring Forth The Hour	38
Your Entrancing Spell	39
Forever Blue	40
The End Of Everything	41
The Rustling Of The Wind	42
Dearest To Truth	43
The Saviour	44
How Soon Is Never	45
The Darker Side	46
The Ancient Pain	47
The Lost Petals Of The Rose	48
Perfect Day	49
The Idyllic Bliss	50
True Love Waits	51
The Ghost In Your Heart And Soul	52
The Universal Pain	53
Doomsday	54
Till Kingdom Come	55
The Godman Of Blood	56
The Godman Of Fire	57
Years Of The Darker Pain	58
In One Song	59
Lost In The Raging Sea Of Memory	60
The Greatest High	61
Upon The Burnished Sky	62
Truth On Your Lips	63
The Day Of Nonesuch Bliss	64
The Scarlet Supremacy	65
The Reign Of God	66
The Death Of The World	67
God Walks Amongst Us Now	68

God Is Born	69
The Day Heaven And Hell Mourned	70
The Greatest Thing	71
The Nobler Finale	72
Ne Plus Ultra	73
Paradise On Earth	74
God And His Bride	75

Ezekiel 7
Isaiah 41:25
John 5:43
Isaiah 45:7
Revelation 13
Psalm 110:1
1 Corinthians 15:28
John 6:45
John 14:28
John 16:12
Zechariah 13:7
Matthew 26:39
Proverbs 8
Matthew 21:33-46
Luke 1:46-55
Isaiah 13:11-13
Isaiah 13:6-10
Isaiah 34:2
Revelation 21:4
Revelation 22:17

This book is dedicated to You.

Acknowledgements

I would like to express my deep sense of gratitude and indebtedness to Dr. Fe Costales, Manuel de los Santos, Judge Simeon Dumdum Jr., Ma. Milagros Dumdum, Jorja Yrastorza, Josemaria Seno, Joseph Brandon Mollaneda, Mathia Gabrielle Erana Ruiz, Sandra Williams, Vicky Farrias and Dr. Ann Clara Alvez whose encouragement, guidance and assistance have contributed immensely to the completion of this book.

The Last War On Earth

The immaculate foretells the universal unrest. Beauty unfolds her credence in secrecy. The Two Messiahs haunt the souls they must test. Through the quaking lands The Two Beasts lacerate human barbarity. The distressing fate rams each hateful place. The Thief prepares the ultimate graveyard of the heartless. The faded sun degenerates through the fading trace. God himself hammers the remorseless. The inculpable forecasts the universal turmoil. Reason unveils her standpoint in mystery. The Two Messiahs hound the souls they must roil. Through the raging seas The Two Beasts mutilate human atrocity. The disturbing spell rends each spiteful state. The Thief provides the conclusive coffin of the ruthless. The bloodied moon deteriorates through the bleeding crate. God himself shatters the relentless. The inviolate foresees the universal despair. Wisdom undrapes her belief in privacy. The Two Messiahs hunt the souls they must dare. Through the storming skies The Two Beasts lacerate human depravity. The deranging lot rips each baneful ground. The Thief presents the eventual tombstone of the soulless. The strangled star disintegrates through the strangling sound. God himself batters the repentless.

The Man Who Set The World On Fire

The word covertly writ his own fate to shapeshift to be me. But the fleeting days were prophesied. He begins to abrade what the eyes revisit to see where ancient gold is magnified. With the shrillest note on the brow the beds were turned down on the red lands. He said: You must attack from the north and wait for me there somehow. Thus trust in destiny which he commands. At night I slumber to never sleep. I only stare at the heavens and dishearten traces. I heard the loudest end time clamor when I was in too deep. The man has disconcerted faces. I notice the shadows waving at me. His question: Is this life pointless and dire? He breathed the same answer compellingly as the man who set the world on fire. He wanders over each horizon for he is lost in his universal kingdom within. In an instant beyond comprehension his control sears the most scarlet sin. At last he found the pale horse not by chance above the devil and his own thorn. You crush lands with termless force. Burn the world for it to be born. None could halt the man and his grit. He breathed the same answer with ire. He claimed the prize for nobody to omit as the man who set the world on fire.

The Supreme Manifesto

On the pernicious road to vehemence the war of reprisal then thrashes as the tempest suddenly crashes. From the seat of ire the holy rebellion overcomes to smack. The perishing sun darkens to black. The darkness looms over the way. I recurrently croon Darker with the Day. Human: Witness the horror present in your mind. Countries eventually crumble in the grind. The boast of humanity is the vain stance. Better leave it to The Certainty of Chance. On the pestiferous path to vengeance the war of requital then invades as the tumult rapidly pervades. From the chair of wrath the divine revolution overturns to blood. The expiring moon bleeds the flood. This is the Judgement of the Bleeding Crown. Mortal: Behold the terror existent in your town. Nations finally collapse in the pang. Dare God himself to destroy the universe by A Bigger Bang. The sanctimonious pride of humankind is his favorite foe. This is The Supreme Manifesto.

The Veredical Marque

In the encircling undermost enmity you must act the part with the unhindered radiant cut heart. Against every despot in the world you should rant like The Philosopher Kant. Born inviolate you tire the fallen leaves burning in the fire. The storm is the thief of such woe. The burned fallen leaves burn me so. Born spotless you tell the broken hearths firing in the shell. The breeze is the chair of such rue. The fired broken hearths fire me too. In the enclosing uppermost amity you must play the role with the unhampered cushion cut soul. Against every tyrant in the world you should fume like The Philosopher Hume. Born immaculate you skin the tattled coves shelling in the din. The squall is the crook of such row. The shelled tattled coves shell me so. Born stainless you save the bidden stones dinning in the rave. The draught is the seat of such hue. The dinned bidden stones din me too.

Bring On The Truth Instead

For every bane there is the boon. For each pain there is the tune. You need to splinter the restlessness of not knowing. For you I would give my life to living. You are the one I am pining for. Life is knocking on your door. You ran away but somehow you drew near. You see death and the dying here. I was predestined to play the lone role. Though the starkness starkened yet still I spared your soul. Ponder upon the mystical memory when hope is dead. Bring on the truth instead. For every right there is the wrong. For each spite there is the song. You need to shatter the restiveness of not seeing. For you I would bid my death to dying. You are the one I am craving for. Death is lying on your floor. You fell away but somehow you came near. You know life and the living here. I was preordained to act the sole part. Though the darkness darkened yet still I saved your heart. Reflect upon the celestial reverie when faith is dead. Bring on the truth instead.

The Pain Of God

To prove to everyone that I shall live thus I crucified myself. There is nothing more to give but the truth you denied yourself. The blood stained the tomb where I slept last night. I walked into the immaculate womb. I shall vanquish in this fight not to make you care. Here comes the darkest hour as the kingdoms of man crumble everywhere. Human empires also lose their power. I shall burn it all with the thought of haunting you. Still you believe in something other. You choose to be Prussian Blue. We are not meant to be I reconsider. There is the perfect place for us I know. This tug-of-war tears your heart. I need not give up and let go even if I must play the gravest part. Somewhere we shall reckon all. For now I must let you drift away. Your path might lead you to fall for me again is what I have to say. Thus time began on the night when I dared to prod. I captained the last flight of the pain of God.

Heroine

The deified rebellion of the catastrophic ire rises in the eventide. The light trails the darkness and tempests on the darkest side. Wisdom is the primordial mysterium who proves her influence. In the holiest verse the intercession unravels her prevalence. The last hour croons the triumphalist song for the scarlet heirs. Providence presents the prism of everything kismet spares. Reason is the primogenial dominium of the universal kingdom. The whole world burns for the innocent to gain the sanctified freedom. The First Messiah unveils his preponderance to the last chosen ones as the cornerstone of ages. The First Beast illustrates through rhyme that overpowers human rages. Beauty is the primeval rosarium on the impending doomsday. In the consecrated revolution theocracy beats to death the disparaging foray. The Second Messiah is the harbinger of lightning. Versus the vilest iniquities The Second Beast commands the striking. The cataclysms ferociously assault with the calamities through the deadliest force. From the smog of dusk until the mist of dawn The Thief lurks with his craftiest source. God himself reigns in the apocalypse with his foolproof master plan. He vanquishes and entombs the doubt and boast of man. Mortal rule is dead and gone for the immaculate who is free from original sin. In the great tribulation the heroine sheds inviolate tears for the mirror of justice to begin.

The Spiteful World

The omnipotent ire annihilates through the sternest countenance. Worldly regimes are strangled vehemently by the supreme rectitude. The universal retaliation is revered with gratefulness by the primogenial presence. The venerable intercessors in mystery allude. The omniscient fury trounces with the deadliest might. The immaculate forewarns with omens that illumine. The inviolable is hailed through the brightest light. The inviolate forecasts the worldwide war and the famine. The hallowed requital strikes down human derision and burns its fate. The crown of twelve stars illuminates for the omnipresent wrath of the interminable. In the sacred eastern oriental southern city the scarlet reign hammers to death the loathsome mortal hate. The venerated prescience foretells the lesson of the end time fable. The sanctified vengeance extirpates the vileness of the culpable mind. The almighty rage eradicates the boast of the cruelest lips. The last hour of reckoning is for the innocent to find. The spiteful world perishes in the apocalypse.

Truth In The Song

I plod on in the sunrise because I have to play the role. For the attainment of the immaculate dream I rise. I have my mind to pole. In the tranquility of the day the sun is high. The great beyond reigns in the ray. It is a pleasure to behold your grin in the golden sky. You irradiate in the sunray. Together we shall be fair. For you I still pray. I have your heart to spare. The geniality of the day clasps the bane and the boon. You are with me today as we hear sooth in the tune. I plow on in the moonbeam because I have to act the part. For the achievement of the inviolate rise I dream. I have my life to start. In the serenity of the night the moon is low. The great unknown rules in the light. It is a treasure to behold your smile in the silver glow. You illuminate in the moonshine. Together we shall be just. For you I still pine. I have your soul to trust. The felicity of the night grasps the weak and the strong. You are with me tonight as we hear truth in the song.

The Birth Of Wisdom

Before the supreme being himself sculpted the timeless celestial phenomenon he created her first in the primeval age. God chiseled the whole universe for the feminine catholicon. She is betrothed to her omnipotent sage. She is imperishable in the predominant grace. The primary companion was none other than Wisdom. The first love story originated from the first embrace. In the universal kingdom God as the king crowned Wisdom as the universal queen to her astonishment. Enchanted she gifted God the fondest moment. Before the supreme being himself inscribed the changeless spiritual magisterium he created her first in the primordial state. God engraved the whole universe for the feminine mysterium. She is engaged to her omnipresent mate. She is indestructible in the predominant stress. The principal companion was none other than Wisdom. The first love story germinated from the first caress. In the universal kingdom God as the king crowned Wisdom as the universal queen to her bewilderment. Enraptured she gifted God the dearest moment.

Heaven Hails Reason

Behold the heretical minds are disintegrated. The disparaging egos perish. The disbelieving tongues are lacerated. The omnipotent wrath conquers to demolish. The almighty eradicates the changeless corrupt life. Mortal rule completely surrenders. The sanctified requital rips the culpable through the condemning strife. The consecrated retaliation crucifies and impales the murderers. The avaricious entrepreneurs are fettered and bankrupted. The hallowed hellion vehemently tramples on the disgraceful tyrants. The abhorrent and the powerless racists are burned and endlessly tormented. The repentless repent fretful amidst the warrants. Nations boast frail weaponry manufactured at a ridiculous buck ten buck fifteen cost. Human evil is beaten to death in the deadliest apocalyptic season. The two messiahs welcome the innocent and the lost. In the bloodiest tribulations stealthily Heaven hails Reason.

Ode To Beauty

You illuminate the universe with the fairest face. In the mystical realm your chaste visage shines. The heavens gifted you the comeliest lace. You lounge in the euphoria with your veracious lines. You irradiate with your celestial presence. The prettiest of all you smile ebullient. Your aspect is amaranthine in essence. You incarnate the empyreal exuberant. Effortless you render the perfect song that you inspirit. You are the embodiment of the feminine divine. You are the quintessence of the daintiest spirit. Creation glistens as you enchant with radiance in your shrine. In the fondest mirth you embrace the paramount sooth. You are the epitome of timeless elegance. You rule with the elysian truth. Totally enraptured everyone in the cosmos reveres your entrancing brilliance.

The End Times

The venerable wind tempests in the midst of the venerated fire. The sacred mass of revelation concelebrates to smite. From oblivion surfaces the sanctified ire. The holy crusade exterminates through its greatest might. The divine vengeance rages in the conquering reprisal. The united two beasts of the apocalypse rule together in the sacrosanct shear. The apocalyptic union summons the consecrated horror in the annihilating requital. The devil himself unleashes Hell this year. The reverent bloodbath splatters in the surest pings. It incises through the strongest heroism for the inculpable. Portentous is the universal church bell that fatally rings. The godliest word beats to death the guilty and the responsible. The blessed mission of Heaven buries the whole world. The creator ravages unwaveringly in the dead of night. The supreme being strikes unfurled. He pours down the ominous purified fuel to the international burning sight. The inviolable begs the maker to eradicate the reign of the sun and the moon. Both degenerate in the bloodstained darkest end. The reverenced vehemence unties the interminable boon. The eternal father pillages the detestable territories of the avaricious and obliterates to upend. In the concluding judgement the innocent hails the surprising victory of the deified rebellion. The inviolate is beholden to the predestined climes. In the celestial conquest the immaculate unveils the true name of the vindicated hellion. Human power shall be stolen by the thief in the end times.

Sapienta

In the vehement purloined mortal hour the Godhead shall reign with predominance in the apocalypse dour. Lord eternally the universe is yours. God himself shall more than just prove to everyone that he exists as the omnipotent force. The strongest realm shall contain the worldwide agony and the rain. Lo and behold in the eradicating era the supreme being shall completely depose empires with Sapienta. In the violent pilfered fatal hour the Godhead shall rule with preponderance in the apocalypse sour. Lord perpetually the universe is yours. God himself shall more than just show to everyone that he exists as the omnipresent source. The greatest state shall reform the worldwide misery and the storm. Lo and behold in the exterminating era the supreme being shall absolutely dethrone kingdoms with Sapienta.

The Lionhearted Principle

In the insufferable pain the omened destiny resigned. Through sincereness you embraced the unbearable state of this mind. I was restrained for the severest reasons. You exhilarated this disconsolate spirit in the comeliest seasons. Ebullience enlivened us in the worldwide rising protest. Evident is the indomitable spirit in the ageless quest. Perceptible in the pining is the inviolate dream. I am beholden to the scarlet teardrops coming on stream. Thus I venerate the immaculate radiance. Through pure endearment the ideal life imparted brilliance. You confessed the forlornest sentiments till the end. In the providential instant there is nothing to rend. You unveiled your candlelit face as the warmest surprise. Enthralled I witnessed the heavens unravel in your amaranthine eyes. Effervescence enlightened us with the brightest hue. The palindrome in the stateliest memory touches you. The sharpest primal scream damaged your chaste intent in the perfect picture card. Nonetheless you hail the universal faith that I revere with utmost regard. I ponder upon the venerable pristineness. I treasure the perpetual piousness. Exuberance emboldened us to surmount evil through the fortitude of the lionhearted principle.

Emptiness Through The Door

Your circle of derision dared to curse. I was indignant at the world for the longest while. I pondered upon the hint of the universe. But once the lone fount of mirth was the smile. Hapless I drowned myself in the abyss. But I came ashore alone to turn down the ominous bed. The hope I hoped against was to submerge you in the deepest bliss. I left the sea with the weary heart above the restive head. The steepest obsession darkened to blankness which I preferred to forgo. Life was prompt in bringing on the vilest tests. You were troubled as well your life almost had to go. I lived on to kill time and its tempests. You sighed in the discouraging misery. Yet still you insisted not to appease but to rage. You repudiated the defiant truth frailly. Fathom the gist on the illustrative page. Your spoiled hatred remains futile in the foray. You have the same ferociousness as the pale moonlight. The sunbeam released the chaste endearment in the sacred city faraway. Sanctimonious pride inflamed the fight. I precluded the vicious cycle of pretension. The scorn you bear for what ensued could be offset. You chant the fundamentalist praises for the illusion. We could meet in the nightfall through kismet. Confess in the darkest hours of your nightmarish fears. On the sanctified ground the verity shall soar. Please concede the genuine reason of your tears. Then disclose your emptiness through the door.

The Drizzle Over The Rain

Are you surprised to see me? I asked you with utmost bliss. You snapped: No because I knew you would do this. At that moment I needed something to rend. That was the melancholiest end. I harkened back to the bane of sheer obsession. You wrenched this disconsolate soul in the harshest fashion. Then bitterly you left after the acridest argument. It was the dreariest disenchantment. In your sternest fury I beheld your remorse as you lied. The sincerest hope disappointedly died. Wretchedly you chose to forget and forgo. Dauntless I damned it all to Hell for you to know. In the loneliest solitude you concealed your glummest doom. I was the principal witness of your darkest gloom. In your sorriest apprehension you repentantly cried. I motioned to Heaven: In the saddest night I repeatedly died. Despondently I was mindful of the severest instant when you were completely torn apart. For your sake be truthful to the genuine pining of your heart. I reckon that together we feel the mistiest recurrent pain. I favoured the drizzle over the rain. I perished because of the gravest desolation. Grimly you disappeared in the forlornest isolation. Defiantly I persisted with the mightiest perseverance just for me to be sane. She is the drizzle and regretfully you are the rain.

The Great Tribulation

There are baneful omens blustering against the lacerated cynics in the vengeful bark. The menacing portents found the disbelievers maimed by the concluding death knell. The dismembered denigrators unsuccessfully attacked the universal faith that was deified by the veridical marque. The butchered detractors languish in the unleashed Hell. The mangled disparagers expire in the doomsday tiff. The tortured blasphemers deservedly vanish. This time fall off the heretical cliff. The identified false and lecherous churches and religions completely perish. God smites the vilest world rulers and seize. The tryst is in the heart of darkness. Heaven prepares its set of keys. The Thief tears down the depraved human rule through the fieriest distress. The end time intercessors batter to surprise. The Two Beasts embolden the innocent through the second coming consolation. The Immaculate enlivens the meek for them to embrace her in paradise. The whole world is burned down in the great tribulation.

DRUNK ON YOUR TEARS

What are your precious secrets that remain unspoken? Why are you repeatedly heartbroken? The worst thing in life is to lose your mind. Yet in the midst of hopelessness it is you I hope to find. When I was on the brink of doom I was not alone in one Hell of a room. Thus I begged God: Is it too much to ask? Does Heaven care about this lonely task? Still I commune in the ecstatic grief of the losing game. Happiness is to hear you speak my name. I figured that my prayers were questioned by God himself to the universe I motioned. Diamonds build castles but what for. Does the narrowest path lead to evermore? I must believe in something whether it blesses or curses everything. Do you also ponder upon the squandered years? I recall being totally drunk on your tears.

The Castle Of Your Heart

We weathered the fiercest storms out in cathedral aisles. The godliest certainty inspirits the universal faith that we share. You revealed the brightest light in your smiles. I relit candles for your sincerest prayer. I hail the merriest instant: It was the loftiest euphoria at first sight. We trysted in the wuthering nightfall together alone. We solemnly plighted our troth in the pale moonlight. I witnessed your holiest state upon the empyreal throne. You proved the elysian truth on your inviolate lips. In the beginning you manifested in the primogenial place. In the wisest instant we finally grasped the zeitgeist of the apocalypse. You bared the perpetual happiness on your immaculate face. The continuance of the purest hope fate has sealed and signed. Divine providence preordained the sacred union since the primordial start. Still the strongest fortress of your mind was surmounted by the vulnerable castle of your heart.

The Liquor Of The Mind

I confess that you are the be-all and end-all. True love never died even after I killed it. For whatever reason at your feet I fall. Frustrated murder was my crime I admit. You chose to brush off my desperation though you also felt so sore. Still I gifted you the radiant cut sanity. The unbearable melancholia is abysmal evermore. Nonetheless you mean each and every nuance to me. The perfect word to write in the paramount song is in the labyrinth of light where we could be lost yet belong. To your lips the twin streams flow. Then and there you taste to find yourself in the afterglow drunk on the liquor of the mind.

Under Starlit Heavens

It is manifest in the darkest curse. It is dead in the buried universe. Find not the fervor here on the earth. I chose to forget the date of its birth. It was broken by the vesper mist. For eons you only needed to be kissed. Regretfully it is missing in oblivion. In the nothingness it was shattered by the wrangling of derision. It perished in the baneful futility. It is lost in the bleakest mystery. No other lips but yours could dispel the reign of the vilest spell. Yet still I gripped the comeuppance with my red right hand. For you I defaced the seven deadly sins in the promised land. But none could feel the lifeless presence but the fiercest rain under starlit heavens.

GOD COMETH

The omen shall scourge on the impending day. The world shall wither and pass away. The famous last words have been said too. Let me introduce the apocalypse to you. The world shall die lonesome in your head for it was written by The True Bread. The world shall croak forlorn in your hand. It shall be done according to his command. The ocean of blood shall rage on the moribund moon. The Thief shall trounce evils with Evil soon. The creeping darkness shall pound the terminal sun. This baleful world shall be dead and gone. The portent shall impale on the upcoming night. The world shall perish and burn so bright. Whom nations dread with the joint breath shall smite with wrath God cometh.

THE DEIFIED ANCESTRY

The sacred rebellion shall creep into the private proverbial head. The two upper hands shall bring around the greatest dread. The whole world shall be burned down in the hallowed reign. The prophesied advent of The Second Beast shall be fulfilled in the eastern bloodied rain. The bleeding moon shall blood human might predestined to be hunted down. The divine revolution shall begin from the blessed oriental southern town. The darkening sun shall darken mortal rule preordained to be absolutely obliterated. The vilest despots shall be completely annihilated. The mortally wounded head shall heal in utero. Lo and behold The Blonde First Beast as the left-handed end time hero. The Two Beasts shall hit to death whoever is in the way in the darkest apocalyptic mystery. The Two Beasts shall eternally dominate in stealth through their deified ancestry.

INTO MY ARMS

The unhindered path astonishes you. The dusk notices your lips. You are inspirited in the cerulean blue. The loftiest dream recurs in ecstatic trips. You light the candle in the moon. Your smile casts the shadow. With bells on I need to be there soon. In transit I must find you in the brightest tomorrow. In the memorable instant I dauntlessly surmise. I venerate the comeliest season manifest in your apparitional eyes. Your sacred tears pour down for the genuine reason. I long to touch your blessed face. The invariable infinite hour is wrapped around your porcelain wrist. I mapped out the heavens in the primordial place. For us I prepared the perfect tryst. Incessantly I yearn for the inviolate unfurled. You unveiled your immaculate charms. I never pray to gain the whole world for you chose to fall into my arms.

Godforsaken

The hounding rays of the sun found me in the forlornest woe. The bleakest severance is the sternest foe. The boundless lamentations left me far more distant than the haunting moon. The merriest nights were seamless for we were obsessively melodized by the perfect tune. The days of paramount mirth were sublimed in the fondest songs beautifully sung. But the chaste whispers vanished when we drifted apart lost and overstrung. Tireless I still treasure your paradisiacal voice which remains totally endearing. The infinite sum of the harshest pain entirely roiled the genuine pining. I walked on endless streets that led to the severest rancour. The unfathomable ocean of our tears is the costliest brand of liquor. We drank each poignant drop of it in the incessant gloom. We were completely distressed in the dreariest doom. I am the repeatedly forsaken and you are the recurrently forgone. The steepest bitterness prefigured your absence before everything was gone. The darkest curse defiantly refused to be forgotten. In the eventual estrangement we were never meant to be godforsaken.

The Apocalyptic Union

The swirling wind through the dying trees is the fatal sign. Using forethought The Second Messiah seethingly elucidates. His apparitional shadow kisses the altar of the shrine. The First Beast creepily appears in every dream that mutilates. Homes everywhere helplessly are drenched in fear. The catastrophic master plan is sealed with the revelations. God sends the deadliest delirium from the sphere. He resolutely annihilates in the nub of mistiness in the severest tribulations. The Second Beast speaks more strident than the loudest thunder. Human dominions are overthrown in the tumult. For each hateful political lie the unanticipated retaliation obliterates the new world order. The parade of bereavement is haunted conclusively by the vastest universal cult. The ancient gallows hound the corners of clouds as cataclysms grip the horizons. The false doctrine of the so-called rapture never occurs. The Thief rises in the requital for foolproof reasons. Scornful dictators are stabbed to death by the omniscient pen that The Lord himself confers. The First Messiah was crucified unscathed in his covert painless death. He lastly blinds and punishes the elect for they only see the sanctimonious sightlessness. The bloodied crown of thorns was his new testament beyond his coached last breath. He overcomes through the mightiest apocalyptic union of light and darkness.

Certain Of His Lent

The spiteful oppressors are bludgeoned in the sacred punishing requital. The supreme being scourges the despicable turncoats through lashings. Behold the fulfillment of the foolproof master plan in the deified dreadful reprisal. The hypostatic union assaults with the severest beatings. The dishonorable disparagers decease hopeless. The malicious bashing partisan tongues are lacerated by the first beast who ferociously inverts. The disgraceful heretics depart headless. The vanishing earth trembles and shakes much earlier than it converts. Venality is crushed and disarticulated too soon. Farewell to the hardhearted for there is one pity pitiless. The holy crusade to hit the culpable is at last the mightiest tune. The creator parades their inglorious deeds which are conclusively heartless. The disdainful detractors are scorched by the vengeful flame. The second beast who was silent all these years has the fiercest ire. The perishing world that tells much of its boast has the detestable name. Human iniquities are obliterated as the culprits deservedly expire. The eternal father incites the hallowed rebellion for the concluding hour is nigh. The prayers of the deceitful are spurned thoroughly. Justifiably the self-righteous fall from the stairway to the vilest lie. The blasphemous denigrators are dismembered methodically. Alas against the sententious beliefs the termless word ignites unrest. Tyrannical governments are obliterated through the omened measure. False doctrines and devious ideologies succumb to the truth who mauls the collective sanctimonious pest. The upper hands writ the kismet of the treasure. The almighty launches the violent retaliation. The determinate paths lead to impartial punishment. The everlasting king accomplishes the purified retribution. He eternally reigns as the noblest taker of life certain of his lent.

Your Face In A Song

In time I found the eyes. Hence I hail the cause. The sacred fire in the skies. Let life clasp its own clause. In time I found the lips. Thus I laud the game. The holy glint in the sips led me to bear each test. I still feel the same. Today I know what is best. In time I found the hands. Hence I cease the search. The solemn gleam in the sands. Let life clamp its own lurch. In time I found the arms. Thus I end the wrong. The blessed flare in the harms led me to dare each state. It was you all along. I never left it to fate. I found your face in a song.

The Resignation Of Love

The comeliest bearing irradiates in the universal kingdom. Often I converse about the silken warbling of your wisdom. I grasp the surges of your lingering dew. Ponder upon your footfalls on the path of the fretless pew. The rim of faith still rises in the crusade of the noble fires. After instants the verve of stealth incessantly suspires. The hellion sets aflame the corruption of history. The storms knead you as the reversal rotates in mystery. The fleeting world of flesh and blood is helplessly frail. The partners of eternal influence treasure the true holy grail. The arrogant empires crumble amongst the fists. The tempest of scrawls is undone by the tightest of wrists. The fiercest book is deified by the celestial beings who fasten. The clemency of the spirit never does hasten. The ring of hope magnifies its reflection and retells this. You bask in the hint of the loftiest bliss. The vision of prudence is sealed by the flapping dove. Fate pleads to us not to tender the resignation of love.

The Immaculate

This is the end of the search for the blessed twin. The symbol of the church is free from original sin. Let the mirror of justice begin. As the morning star you are the queen of the heart. Full of grace you are undefiled from the start. Let the seat of wisdom impart. You are inviolate and faithful. You are inviolable and merciful. You are pure perpetually. Thus you are immaculate for eternity. This is the end of the quest for the cause of joy and boon. The vessel of honour wears the crest and the crown over the moon. Let the house of gold commune. You are clothed with the sun as the queen of the soul. You are the venerable one prudent from the pole. Let the gate of heaven extol. You are inviolate and faithful. You are inviolable and powerful. You are chaste perpetually. Thus you are immaculate for eternity.

The Bloodiest Eclipse

Behold the arrival of the supreme being. He prepares in stealth the last emperor. The first beast obliterates the disparaging. He ferociously expunges as the conqueror. He harkens back to eons of bane. Witness the paradoxical fulfillment of terror. He unmasks the godliest pain. From the core of darkness comes the horror. The bitter moon and the acrid sun perish in the bloodiest eclipse. The last emperor is the chosen one. The second beast hankers for the immaculate and her inviolate lips. Then he puts to death the sanctimonious scriptural tone. He annihilates human vileness. His footsteps lead to her blessed moan. He burns down the world in the dimness. He passes by the wall of the dead. God himself had Jesus Christ crucified thus it was done. The location of the crux of punishment is in his stead. The supreme being is the last emperor and the prodigal son. He tramples on mortal despots in the apocalypse. He reigns with vengeance in the bloodiest eclipse.

Beauty Like Death

I am near you to stand from afar. I hope to share the wind to bar. You dwell in the hearth and the hue. I close my eyes only to see you. I need not the reason nor the chance. I witness your elusive stance. The grace deals with the past. Your immaculate glow is recast. Along fate I bid the possession. Craft then treasure the illusion. I feel the room where you breathe. There is the sphere dying underneath. You raise existence now dead. Cleave the lone face you dread. Are you here to tug my breath? Bask in your beauty like death.

Ace Of Pain

The impending eventide shrouded the holiest trail. Within the disconsolate heart the immaculate persisted to unveil. The inviolate in secret wailed in anguish under the clandestine skies. The unbearable wretchedness magnified the bloodshot eyes. In the blustery weather the ominous unanticipated presence surfaces. Predestined there are two recently deified birthplaces. The mortal head wound of the blonde first beast of burden healed in the stealthiest truth. The prodigal sons reign together in the godliest sooth. The funeral of the sanctified innocence strikes to death the heretical disposition. The catholicon disarticulates the unbelievers in the great tribulation. The mysterium dismembers the disparaging assailants in the concluding year. The lithest tangent lips kissed the venerated scarlet tear. The treasure is concealed inside the universal mind. The apocalypse is fulfilled in the doomsday grind. Fate concluded to pour the fiercest rain. The second beast of burden becomes the ace of pain.

The Thief In The Night

I endured as the forsaken and the forgone. If you have nobody else to love then I am the forgotten one. The melancholies stir the resolution but I shall be there for you. Steadfast I remain obdurate with the clue. Still your concealed tears fall on the testament. Heaven summons you to decisively repent. All the while I am the one you truly dread. The truth is there revealing your secrets in the universal stead. You abhorred me with the purest ire in the forlornest mess. Totally gripped you grieved in the harshest distress. Let us end the estrangement and regain the loftiest high. I identified the chaste sentiment to comfort your regretful sigh. I roamed and revolved to witness the sacred betrothal. Nullity unraveled in the celestial wretchedness of the betrayal. The riveting fact is not your ubiquitous absence. Conclusively I shouldered the false reason of your elusive presence. I became familiar with every bit of you so soon. You sang for me the perfect tune. I crooned for you before in the sunniest light. In the darkness I stole your heart as the thief in the night.

The Most Beautiful Song

Together we pondered upon the most beautiful song. To me you articulated with effortless eloquence yearlong: It beautifully intones the melancholiest regard of all. I rejoined: For your wondrous riposte again I fall. You stated: I reckon that you favoured me. I declared: But I perished in the ecstasy. I elucidated: In truth I intended to set you free as well. You replied: I know your life was consumed by Hell. You wept: This is the forlornest account. I reasoned: Be not afraid to lose the given fount. You held: You untied us from the obsession. I pressed: I shaded you in the throes of passion. You recalled: From the first fight to the last cry. I interrupted: It was what love meant to die. You dimmed: Before the lone hope was to forgo. I held your hand: Your tears are the genuine reason not to let go. You remarked: The end of the affair caused us to be so marred. I darkened: Bitterly you left broken and scarred. You sighed: I weep in vain let us forget about it. I ached: I beg to differ for I know your secret. I pleaded: Confess how misery pelted you too. You wist with pain: I am so tired of being true. Then you stressed: Please do not get this wrong. I hinted: You do eclipse the most beautiful song.

Trampling On Fate

The end time rebellion shatters human rule. The genuine purpose of life is lost on the disparaging fool. I found you on a dog day afternoon. You sang the perfect tune. I squandered the chance in the omened plot. You scampered away from our lot. You were daunted by my conviction. For the atonement I saved you in the mission. The ancient fairy tale has the definitive title. It spins around the immaculate recital. I brave the wearisome strife. Still I ponder upon the eternal life. You witnessed how I roiled the vow. Doomsday surfaces in the apocalypse now. Your tinted lips snapped with the celestial pain. I hounded you in the tiresome strain. The primal reason for us to be together is late. Yet let us regain the purest happiness through trampling on fate.

Bring Forth The Hour

Beyond horizons I looked for the care. Through sunsets I searched for you there. The misfortune remains for you have never appeared. The imparted miracle soon disappeared. You did shroud in the shadow of the blues. With the beauty of the whole world gone in hues. Still you convey efflorescence in your supernal eyes. Sonancy escorts your own sacerdotal ties. Yet your absence gives me no other choice. Nonetheless sonority shepherds your impeccable voice. Withal inflorescence stresses your inimitable face. I long to be the witness of your amaranthine grace. I was enamoured in the lowest silence. I am the fool to embrace in the vain insistence. To never grasp you is the disconsolate tear. Bring forth the hour you would appear.

Your Entrancing Spell

No radiance but yours illuminates the dappled night. Beyond the blankness of the mind without time. The moon whimpers over its fatal plight. Hateful is the movement of the sanctimonious clime. The stars opt to decease and greet their demise. The seas welcome death across the diffuseness of the bleakest misery. Yet still I see the gleam in your undaunted eyes. Your monument is clandestine as the final mystery. The whole world is about to perish in your arms. The vanishing ground encroaches the failing sands. I tightened the recapitulation of your charms. Behold there are more than two holy lands. The expiring skies pour down the repentant woe. You speak the word that upends the bleats of fire. The sun writhes at long last as the conquered foe. The latter tears of mankind bleed in the mire. Upon the cliff God himself shall build his kingdom. Your chants pare the disappearing winds of Heaven and Hell. At length the innocent gain the consecrated freedom. I heed and parcel the call of your entrancing spell.

Forever Blue

The sky with its hues could be cruel in the grind. The wind with its squalls could also be unkind. You desperately need to be heard by someone. You make it through the night but appears no one. The moon with its beams could be cold so beware. The sun with its rays could hound you anywhere. Each day at a time you do your best. Yet still you often you grumble that you are not so blessed. The air with its drafts could rouse something you dread. The sea with its waves could leave you for dead. In your solitude you spurn the world the legend sold in his song. With the love of your life gone things could go wrong. The star with its dusts could stress what is in vain. The land with its clefts could brush off your pain. The bottom line is you just have to pull through. Persevere in your forlorn existence though you seem forever blue.

The End Of Everything

Never have I been addicted this way. I know others get dependent too. The certain high insists to stay. I care not if I lose control over you. I feel the sting now as I look upon your face. I do my best for us somehow. Addiction hits with such disgrace. It is foolish to call your name. Withal on perfect days it can kill. As of late the pang is the same. The story of my life becomes nil. By no means have I craved more for show. There must be the genuine reason to gain. This obsession for you I let go. I nearly lost all to the olden pain. I am here to right each wrong. You stonily deny so I choose to regretfully sing. This could be the farewell song and the end of everything.

The Rustling Of The Wind

Venerate the scarlet tears that rage in the fiercest flood. Revere the holy crusade as the moon turns into blood. Live on in the crux of time and defy until last day. Erupt and conquer for the eternal reign and slay. Endure everything in the fourteen stations of distress. The whole world perishes in the presence of omnipotent greatness. Hail the pertinent life and the sacred revolution. Thrive through the cuts and thorns in the blessed rebellion. Rescind the last breath of the merciless. In an instant sever human vileness. It is crucial in burning falsehoods for you to labour and to lacerate. Surmount mortal evil and mutilate. Honour the divine alliance as the sun darkens in the dimness. Prevail in the final hour to engrave the shrouded hellfire in the darkness. Vanquish the iniquities that scourged and sinned. Bring down oppressive dominions in the rustling of the wind.

Dearest To Truth

Your principles ought to be freed. The corruptible society refuses to share. Lose your pretensions and greed. Through the reason of fortune you care. There is the pain that stops at nothing. Your hope dissipates as you delay. The nature of life still is grueling. You are surrounded by the pretentious crowd bound to decay. Ponder upon your furtive verve and beam. Be untied dissimilar to the vain. Hold on to your genuine dream. Let your tears flow in the rain. Your anguish defers the grace. Integrity leads to salvation writ to soothe. Bear it out with the upfront face. Reconsider that you are dearest to truth.

The Saviour

The Saviour sets the world on fire. He revisits the places that illumine. His precision outstrips the post meridian ire. He trails the traces of the pang and the famine. His blood quenches the thirst for the final war amidst the lassitude. His forbearance overturns the fiercest defiance. He brings around his wistful fortitude. He incites the rebellion with his presence. He lacerates derisions at his gate. He perseveres with wisdom that in tongues riddle. In the comeliest towns his arms throbbed as of late. Remembrance leads him into the tinges of the doomsday fable. Though he causes the deadliest cataclysm in the encomium still he basks in it. The time has come for him in varying heights to be the knave. Rather than spend it in seclusion he lets the last day devour the elect and their merit. He magnifies what truly levelled the whole world to the grave. If I were The Saviour then I have no one but you to save.

How Soon Is Never

I elucidate for everyone more accursed. There is the purified ill unrehearsed. Regretfully morose were you in your eye. At night the worst tempest rises to die. Behold the kingdom that ushers in doom. I wish you saw me in the gloom. After eons then I shall lead. Resentfully you pointed out yourself: I do bleed. You lasted for the dead inevitably. Your lips are cold in the melancholy. While nothing deemed but haste. It was your kiss I longed to retaste. Wrath has the meaning yet I spent. In an instant I lost your element. The reflecting hour is torn apart. For your sake rip your deceitful heart. Withal baneful I lose: O Bitter. The foiling: How soon is never.

The Darker Side

The heavens speak dotingly about you. I prod the sacred heart to tremor. At high noon the sun saves everything true. At the banquet your timed lip is bitter. Let your cheeks be tameless on the ground. At the end of the dusk the glory brightens. The skies form the portrait without the sound. Horizons raze as the cherished brow lightens. In turn the crown of thorns rips the lair. Your eyes squint beneath the glove. The moon permeates the mirage through its stare. The stars pained to proffer the rebellious love. The voice you freed is on the cliff alone. Your tongue of fire is deemed too hallow. The almighty casts the first stone. In the storm there is the darker side to follow.

The Ancient Pain

The light illumines what the spirit sustains. The true language of the soul immovably refrains. It shall never be ensnared by the corrupt concept. The fleeting schemes expire because of the fraudulent precept. I have in me the witness that sees all. I shall tear down the prevalent pretentious social wall. Through the inducement I did unlearn. I walk with dedications that shall burn. The minds full of misused ill increase. Earth shall be brought to its knees. What I desire is much more than that. I reflect upon freedom from pain as I tip my hat. I dauntlessly risk everything only to get it done. The truth is you shall lose me to none. You nobly pine and long though you restrain. The olden door of your heart shall disclose the ancient pain.

The Lost Petals Of The Rose

Lost is the face beneath the sun. Behold the radiance of the sunset that enshrouds the mystically gone. Lost is the smile under the moon. Behold the splendour of the moonrise that enfolds in the cardinal tune. Lost is the voice below the star. Behold the brilliance of the stardust that enclasps the ethereally far. Lost is the touch nether the sky. Behold the grandeur of the skyline that entwines in the paramount high. In celestial throes count the lost petals of the rose.

Perfect Day

I have the second wind in me. I once let you go and set you free. But now I behold your immaculate face. And you are ecstatically blushing because of the comeliest lace. Before we needed time for us to run. La dolce vita has truly begun. This is the supreme surprise. I am witnessing the utmost elation in your eyes. With your inviolate voice you sing with sheer radiance in this sacred oriental southern queen city. You are inviolable and blessed for eternity. We are here to share the brightest tomorrows. This is the crowning end so pack up your sorrows. From my inmost the greatest high elevates. We reach the loftiest of the writ states. Let us forget about the severest pain. We embrace with the strongest candor for we have the whole universe to regain. To our provenance we found the way particularly on this perfect day.

The Idyllic Bliss

The truth beneath your blessed eyes is your venerable paradise. The hidden treasure of your private universe is the perfect place that lifted the darkest curse. The mystery of your fairest face beams the brightest light I retrace. Your sightliest bearing entrances the provenance where I first caressed your undefiled essence. The inviolate intent communed with the sincerest hope enraptured as the towing rope. Your mystical rose is the comeliest. Its spotless beauty is reverenced as the purest. Below your loveliest cheeks is the chaste spring. I am the witness of the inviolable longing. Your immaculate lips which God tasted in the primordial kiss perpetually illumines the idyllic bliss.

True Love Waits

Teardrops bleeding on the stream. Nightmarish becomes the recurrent dream. From the crust the morning of unhappiness is disturbing you. Bloodied you vanished into the blue. But the trailer follows you wherever you run. Haunted by horror your doomsday has begun. The bloodshot eyes of the pursuer bleeds for more. The afternoon of loneliness is distressing you from the core. The ominous presence surrounds you as you weep. Hounded by terror you found yourself in too deep. The prowler you truly fear is Evil at its kindest state. The Devil is in the detail and he stands at your gate. The evening of dreariness is disquieting you from the mantle. You trusted the lurker who appeared to be gentle. He was forbidden to be with you by The Fates. Thus he fled Hell to surprise you for true love waits.

The Ghost In Your Heart And Soul

The amaranthine star you cast down haunts the remorseful frown. Heaven is the spectator of your firing hand. The clutch is still the searing stand. Each single tumultuous night you slip in the moonlight. Hell is the onlooker of your flaming nape. The clasp is still the stripping drape. The universe shall hear it soon. I must put out the illuminated moon. Unremitting am I for I play the primordial role as the ghost in your soul. The labyrinthine sky you cast out hounds the regretful doubt. Heaven is the observer of your flashing face. The grasp is still the splitting trace. Each single tempestuous day you trip in the sunray. Hell is the bystander of your flaring hair. The grip is still the shedding lair. The universe shall see it done. I must put down the irradiated sun. Unrelenting am I for act the primeval part as of the ghost in your heart.

The Universal Pain

The tidal resonance shrouded the obsession of the glistening sea. You once implored forgiveness because of the bidden soul I see. You wept secretively under the clandestine skies. The unbearable anguish taunted your enflamed eyes. I am in the absence of greatness that comes from above. On the frangible lands I mourned the death of our love. The feral wind of nil change has lost another one in someplace else where you could hear none. The holiest word bleeds the worst strain. With many a hopeful verse still seemingly I have nothing to gain. What I whispered fell on blindfolded ears. It is finished though I prefer not to forget about the discarded yesteryears. Thus the abandoned happiness equaled the harshest strife. This indomitable spirit shall never be distraught by the vilest tribulations of life. The celestial omens heartened me to trample on the debilitating fears. These tangent lips melancholically tasted the last drop of your tears. For the world to know with sheer earnestness I die to care. Beneath the luminous stars I grieved over the end of the affair. You traded your wishes in the tearful rain. The treasure is hidden in the universal pain.

Doomsday

The impending doomsday incites universal turmoil. The fellest rain is the weeping rose. It has bloodied thorns that wound and roil. I wait for the largest cosmic bleeding so it goes. The apocalyptic answer to prayers remains invariable withal. In the loneliest end time instant reconsider everything. The celestial omens point to the final fall. The secrets for failure are significant before the second coming. The cross is inverted in the great tribulation. The requital is without and within. The global unrest originates from the divine eastern oriental southern revolution. The inviolate is not beholden to the original sin. Mortal dominions lament as they are being burned. In the last war the guilty are defaced in the concluding year. After eons the culpable are deservedly mutilated and spurned. Human impunity is dismembered by the scarlet immaculate tear.

Till Kingdom Come

The doomsday winds vehemently rage. Human rule is beaten to death in the deadliest age. The disparaging heretics are thrashed in the hallowed rebellion. The disbelieving heathens are trampled upon by shrouded hellion. For the innocent watch the unlit trips. Wring the tears to fall on these lips. Baneful is the demise of the partisan unbeliever. The final day is up to the upper hands to smother. The omen changed from the bleeding hue. Farewell to the political lie as the scornful dictators perish in the rue. You remain resentful with the hints. I close doors and windows with the quints. I saved the endearment in the fair game. We silenced each other by bedevilling the old flame. Fate was sealed in the killing moon. I set you free for the intended boon. Ponder upon where I am coming from. Stay stern and tacit till kingdom come.

The Godman Of Blood

The descending darkness spreads as the hour of reprisal falls. Instantly the horrible light blasts from the sky. Thus the fiercest wrath shatters merciless prosperous walls. The tyrannical dominions bleed and die. The vengeance of The Godman trounces in the dark. His judgement annihilates the doubt and boast of man. The crusade of Hell soars with the burning mark. The blisters of fire and brimstone destroy within the master plan. The terrible fate of the culpable is deservedly chained. The chastisement obliterates the baneful wealth of strength. Heaven revolts against humanity and its greed which is stained. The concluding day is done at length. The Godman burns the sphere of power and gold. Versus the circle of human rule ravages the fatal night. From oblivion the holiest fury devastates the world bought and sold. Into ashes and straight to dust the mortal might. In the mire rises the bloodiest flood. Behold The Godman of Blood.

The Godman Of Fire

The torn immaculate desolately weeping. The inviolable bleeding Mother Mary. Jesus Christ died on the cross with the psalm of eternity. He vanished in the basest rue. Crucified for you in the scourging state sealed by the harshest fate. The Prince who drank the evermore is now The King you adore. But he came to release his ire. He reigns ceaseless as The Godman of Fire. The worn inviolate despondently mourning. The incorruptible grieving Mother Mary. Jesus Christ died on the cross with the hymn of infinity. He perished in the vilest rue. Crucified for you in the plaguing plot signed by the hardest lot. The King who drank the everclear is now The God you endear. But he came to unleash his ire. He rules endless as The Godman of Fire.

Years Of The Darker Pain

The most perfect angel was cast down. Jesus Christ himself was crucified. What is it all about? I asked the clown. He said: I loved her so but she died. I do my best but nothing does happen. Yet with all my might I carry the cross. The lonely wreck I have become is now the forsaken. Even time with friends worsens the loss. The stone cold Heaven might not care. In my darkest hours I called the name. The person refused to answer so there. Now I am left the sore loser in the losing game. Yet I would rather fall again and lose. I shall weather the fiercest rain. I am the fool for it is still you I choose through all the years of the darker pain.

In One Song

If you were to leave with a distant mind then map out where you must go to find who dimmed the glint in your spent eyes. Consider the absence of many a surprise. This instant you reckon that something is truer than your loneliness as years get lonelier. Your solitude brought you to your knees and made you plead: O Heaven please. From your heart of stone where pain sits comes your disavowal yet misery revisits. What you did repudiate in front of a face is haunting you so in a communal place. When you ceased to spark your dying spell died as you sang the line: I forgot to tell. Confess your secret care that you have treasured long. Let yourself sing your tell-all in one song.

Lost In The Raging Sea Of Memory

The raging sea without forbearance drowned the dimmer part I possess. Indomitably I endured the submersion for I enthused to redress. I pondered upon our inaugural embrace. The merriest years that trailed in resplendence I retrace. Without forewarning we creeped into the private walls of mystery. The foremost shimmering of Heaven I treasured with gratefulness in the ecstasy. We trysted in the lustrous sky with the fragranced air. In the midst of the loneliest doldrums everything else failed to compare. The loftiest elation engraved the innocent blush. Your illumined presence is the cause for this enamoured heart to rush. I lurked with the wuthering wind that led to the crepuscular grain of sand. Then the dead calm waves caressed my inspirited feet as I grasped your labyrinthine hand. I indulged ebullient in the comeliest pipedream you magnificently painted for me. Soaked in the utmost mirth beyond what the tinted eye can see. But in the bitterest instant you vanished into the blue that I dauntlessly crossed. Without the surest aim I steered this disquieted soul to haste into oblivion fretless at the steepest cost. The tenuous tide rose from the cerulean sleep. It crashed the restiveness of this mind buried unfathomably deep. Estranged thoughts reverberated the disappointment in the mist of the sleepless night. In the haunting questions I wearingly deemed for the enlightened answers were out of sight. I was crestfallen when you eluded the melancholiest goodbye. I was totally disenchanted even though I never let the lone chaste hope die. The pitiless abyss swallowed the nethermost dysphoria till the darkest side of me was born. I gasped the last breath as I was completely worn. Still I persisted to obtain the paramount relief in the purest light of day. For the sheer sorrowfulness the fondest shore had something real to say. I regained solace through the greatest resilience. The universe between us lit the eternal radiance. Tranquil I returned to the origin of every me. Faraway lost in the raging sea of memory.

The Greatest High

The greatest high I have overcome. The whole world shall turn till kingdom come. It was foretold I need to get sedated. You treated me with the caustic silence that I hated. Forget about it. You are cursed not to care. I just had to quit too to make it fair. Better off with Jesus Christ? Should you forsake me again I would not be surprised. The teetotal life is more worthwhile than your most addictive smile. The doomsday unfolds the end. In the apocalypse now you stonily pretend. Yet you shall always be the perennial heroine. For you I remain genuine. But I have not told you why. You are even greater than the greatest high.

Upon The Burnished Sky

In the midst of the dreariness you weep alone. Secrets manifest in your bloodshot eyes. You shield the reason of your heart of stone. The truth is evident in your isolated cries. I live unseen within your walls. I determine who I really am to you. But you make it seem so false. Thus your private tears betray you too. Nonetheless I listen to our torch song. Timeworn I invigorate the urgency of us. I am emboldened as I engrave to right each wrong. You languish alongside the coastal fuss. In your solitude you ask the heavens about being lonely. You need not waste another year. Everyone has also felt weariness and misery. The vanishing point: I am still here. For our sake I needed to endure the drabbest strife. We must be set to lose it all. There was I musing on life. Then and there for you I fall. The recurring dream: We lit the old flame till the fieriest dawn. Through time stars have rewritten our fate. In the infinite hour the dusk was magnificently drawn. Your confessional whisper is never late. The gamble with diamonds might surprise you. I would not ruin the nth chance for us to try. This hope of mine: The dimness to its blue. Yet we could run into each other upon the burnished sky.

Truth On Your Lips

For you to lift the ancient curse you need courage to unveil your passion for me. We shall be astounded beyond the splendour of the universe. Let us enfold the paramount testament of eternity. For you to rule out the romance you need to admit with absolute certitude that you are the mere friend. Then I shall endure it with fortitude. I shall never heave in anguish in the end. For you to break the spell of the enchantment you need to uphold with conviction that you have no longing to confess. Then I shall accept it with composure and wish you well. I shall let you go with the last caress. But for you to reveal in all honesty you need valor to divulge that I was always in your mind. We shall be astonished beyond the magnificence of the cosmos and its beauty. Let us embrace the cardinal covenant of providence and leave the severest pain behind. Still your impeccable elegance grips. I shall hear the truth on your lips.

The Day Of Nonesuch Bliss

We were bound for the purest happiness. I grew up together with the totality of merriness. I welcomed hearths that sparked within me. I clutched them for scores fruitfully. I tasted your lithest upper lip that stays as lyrical as this harmonious trip. I lay in wait under your skies. In an instant we conversed about chromatic eyes. I have reveries that I shall surely return to soon. The tangled song enriched me with the tangent tune. The stateliness of the world with its pull is shaded by that way you stun in full. I am still cherishing that moment. Our reunion at the perfect tryst led to our atonement. We lifted the curse resolutely with the kiss. Life was at its lushest on the day of nonesuch bliss.

The Scarlet Supremacy

Let me reintroduce the apocalypse. He butchers the disparaging lips. He hits to slay human evil. He overcomes in the upheaval. With his upper hand he conquers to reign. He entombs the vilest mortal iniquities in the bloodiest rain. The blasphemous false religions along with the counterfeit churches and unbelief are deservedly struck down. He rises from the prophesied eastern oriental southern town. He assails in the worldwide unrest. He hunts down the culpable in his divine quest. Impunity is tormented in the darkness. Worldly dominions expire in the dimness. He has each angel and every saint at his back. From the north he surmounts to attack. He has kingdoms and empires to finally shatter. He has regimes and dictatorships to lastly batter. His true love is The Scarlet Woman born as Maria. He rebuilds the third temple and rules as The Scarlet Messiah.

The Reign Of God

    The recurrent arcane portent is the reason for God to crucify. He hammers the despicable despots for earthly tyrannies to die. In the dead of night human rule deceases with the baleful guilt. The First Messiah plays his greatest role up to the hilt. God annihilates above all the pitiless leaders. The vilest iniquities are obliterated by his vengeance initially in fetters. The Second Messiah cuts down the disdainful collective culpable head. His impaling word is universally dreaded. In the apocalypse each mortal without scruples is spent. The disbelieving lips fear to whisper the name of The First Beast in his lent. The celestial omens spread as he exhales. The interminable grips the basest lies of the end time tales. God tears down autocracies and regimes in the worldwide perishing breath. He batters the deceitful international peace accord to death. His ire hits the mightiest boast in the triumphalist tune. He eradicates erroneous ideologies and false doctrines with the irrefutable boon. From the north The Thief attacks every merciless sod. The disdainful heretics are infirm and paltry cowards in the presence of God. From crevices to coves the virtuous behold the brightest light. The bleeding of the moon and the darkening of the sun emanate from the sole divine might. The Second Beast has the sternest countenance that creeps nightmarishly in dreams. He punishes the blameworthy and exterminates their spiteful schemes. The Second Messiah scorches hateful lands not in vain with the craftiest face. In retaliation against the devious speeches the graves are in place. The primogenial ire rises from his omnipresent eyes. God conquers in his reign with the deadliest surprise.

The Death Of The World

Predestined the world shall end in the dimmest state. God grips the impending fate. Impunity shall be mutilated for the pitiless to know. Witness the whole universal show. You shall see the vanquishing today. The world shall die on the last day. The world dead in the dimness shall be reborn in the harshest pain. The ire of God brings about his eternal reign. The world shall perish in the devastation. God shall tear down kingdoms in the revolution. Till the last breath God shall throttle the whole world to death. Preordained the world shall end in the darkest plot. God grasps the portending lot. Iniquity shall be lacerated for the merciless to know. Witness the whole universal show. You shall see the conquering tonight. The world shall die on the last night. The world dead in darkness shall be reborn in the brightest light. The wrath of God brings about his immortal right. The world shall perish in the demolition. God shall burn down empires in the retribution. Till the last breath God shall strangle the whole world to death.

God Walks Amongst Us Now

If I were the creator of the universe I would relinquish my own divinity. I would brave the curse and involve myself in human misery. But if I may have this: The hope to find the nuance of every soul and mind. Then for the world the seas shall glimmer exhilaration for us. Everyone shall clasp the sublime and the wondrous. If I were the ruler of the universe I would cope with the perils and face how life could be unfair. I would live powerless and immerse myself in the debilitating mortal despair. But if I may have this: The want to lead as the plenitude if anyone should ever plead. Then for the world the stars shall glitter ebullience for any of you. Jubilate for Empyrean has the clue. If I were the creator of the universe I would deal with the challenges. I would have the prophesied destiny that could be adverse. Still I would cherish existence for ages. But if I may have this: The wish to win the nicety of every smile and grin. Then for the world the lands shall flutter exaltation for us. Everyone shall grasp the divine and the marvelous. If I were the ruler of the universe I would endure the pain and the suffering as my sacrifice. I would have the predicted fate that could be worse. I would struggle amidst the living who play dice. But if I may have this: The need to deem as the plethora if anyone should ever dream. Then for the world the skies shall flicker effervescence for any of you. Exuberate for Elysium has the cue. The paramount apocalyptic message is: Everyone shall overcome everything somehow. Behold the ultimate surprise: God walks amongst us now.

God Is Born

During the nativity of the mightiest seer seven eclipses decked the heavens in his birth year. The comet stayed watchful around the span to witness the parturition of the greatest man. He purchases the whole world and sets it on fire. He fulfills the primogenial vehemence and the primordial ire. The moon bleeds as he burns human boast and lets it die. The sun darkens as he crushes mortal dominion and its despicable lie. The lands quake as he hammers the cruelest traitors. The seas rage as he crushes the vileness of the disparagers. The skies storm as he annihilates the culpable. Earthly tyrannies wither as he reigns as the interminable. He rises to bring around the upper hand. He emanates from the eastern oriental southern land. But the blameless never taste death. He delivers the providential equitable breath. Alas through his fiercest vengeance false doctrines and erroneous ideologies are torn down. He attacks from the north and assails in every town. He vanquishes the wickedness of global rulers. He overcomes the evils of international leaders. Lo and behold he walks amongst the living. He has the sole divine might to end everything. But he spares the innocent who are careworn. At last beyond good and evil God is born.

The Day Heaven And Hell Mourned

The stars grieved when he was born. It was the day he became The Son. Heaven and Hell were completely torn. Yet the climate was spun. The winds wailed when he was born. Everything was set in the master plan. The roles were reversed with the baneful thorn. It was his time to be The Immortal Godman. The skies wept when he was born. It was the day he became The Child. Heaven and Hell were entirely worn. Yet the weather was mild. The seas wailed when he was born. Everything was laid in the master plan. The roles were reversed with the baleful scorn. It was his time to be The Eternal Godman.

The Greatest Thing

The greatest thing trounces the vilest pain. The strongest storm pours down the fellest rain. The mercy of God conciliates the righteous souls and honours the innocent roles. The darkened sun darkens the fretful eyes. The First Messiah rewards the labours of the illustrious and the impoverished through his patrician surprise. The divine revolution eruptively surfaces with the deadliest beginning. The wrath of God throttles false human belief and strangles wrong mortal reasoning. The chameleonic sky displays omens to the world in its plight. In time embrace the darkest side of light. The created beings still tread on dissimilar pathways to certainty. The First Beast in truth leads creation to eternity. To everyone in the cosmos this I must stress: The blood along with the sweat and the virulence of tears are the keys to everlasting peace and happiness. The Second Beast untangles the conclusive burdensome crusade that you unexpectedly believe. The Second Messiah comes with his own name that the chosen ones receive. The bloodied moon bleeds in the perilous hour of reckoning. God and his Bride inaugurates the universal salvation which is the greatest thing.

The Nobler Finale

The unanswered questions remain puzzling. Behold the answers are forthcoming. For the wrong and the right: The legitimate answer shall be in plain sight. The depraved and the holy shall find wisdom in solidarity. Everyone should pull together for this song. The better end shall not be long. The unsolved problems remain baffling. Behold the solutions are upcoming. For the poor and the rich: The equitable solution shall be in perfect pitch. The light and the darkness shall find reason in impartialness. Everyone should pull together for this tune. The nobler finale shall be soon.

Ne Plus Ultra

The greatest goal of the universal mission heralds the predestined victory. I treasure the forbearing covenant of immortality. The fruition of the noblest dream springs from the innermost core. It is magnified by the rending sound of evermore. I once lived with the ominous presence. I am beholden to the primogenial immaculate resplendence. Creation declares its collective gratefulness. Everyone celebrates in the everlasting happiness. The first step to find Heaven and its key to everything begins with the cosmic exulting. The will to power is the thrust of the strongest might. Dare I state that I thrive on it each day and night. To urge you to confess at last: You have won my heart. It is the song of songs and the genuine reason of art. I summon everyone to hail the primordial quest. Behold the world set on fire as God does the rest. This indomitable spirit was born of the severest adversity. Thus I proclaim the ne plus ultra of triumphs in history.

Paradise On Earth

The remuneration shall be manifest in paradise. The miracle shall be unraveled in verse. The universal conquest shall arise. The godliest crusade shall bless each curse. The immortal bliss shall guide us to the eternal life. In the harvest there shall be no need for us to fear. In the grave of anguish and strife: At last everyone is here. The reconciliation shall be evident in paradise. The oracle shall be untangled in song. The universal triumph shall surprise. The holiest mission shall right each wrong. The eternal mirth shall steer us to the immortal glow. In the fruitage there shall be no need for us to care. In the tomb of pain and sorrow: At last everything is fair.

God And His Bride

In the beginning before God created the cosmos he created her first. Creation figures that in her love for the creator she has the perpetual thirst. For her inviolate affection she need not throw the coin into the primogenial wishing well. Her immaculate voice rings the universal church bell. Full of grace she has eternity to consider. God disguised as someone else is her redeemer. He blessed her with the promised land. In her recurrent dream she held him in the proverbial grain of sand. In her darkest hour she longed to say: I remain smitten by the brash entity who went his own way. In the rue she sheds blood through her apparitional eyes for the primal woe. For her immortal beloved she endures as the lady we all know. She is enraptured though for the severest reason she felt forsaken. In tears she renders the perfect song as her sincerest prayer for everybody to be forgiven. The primordial rulers with their eternal influence reign together. The genuine purpose of life is in their hands for whomever. Both save the world as it was written in the holiest verse. God venerates the queen of the universe. Witness the omnipresent union attained in one kiss. God left Heaven and Hell for her to be his. She has the truest pining in her heart and mind. The man who turned into the second beast is the saviour she needs to find. The plot thickens for the wordsmith foretold without miss. God and his bride celebrate in the stateliest wedded bliss.

CPSIA information can be obtained
at www.ICGtesting.com
Printed in the USA
BVHW031049051219
565738BV00005B/31/P